THE DROWNING BOY'S GUIDE TO WATER

THE
DROWNING
BOY'S
GUIDE
TO WATER

Cameron Barnett

Autumn House Press

Pittsburgh

Autumn House Press receives state arts funding support through a grant from the Pennsylvania Council on the Arts, a state agency funded by the Commonwealth of Pennsylvania, and the National Endowment for the Arts, a federal agency.

Cover Photograph: Alamy.com
Book and cover design: TG Design

ISBN: 978-1-938769-26-9
Library of Congress Control Numer: 2017944869

TABLE OF CONTENTS

I

When the Mute Swans Return *11*

Nonbinding Legislation, or a Resolution *12*

To the Octopus *14*

Purple Ruckle *16*

Stack *18*

Stepping into Your Mouth *19*

Country Grammar *20*

True Facts About Water *22*

Letter to Sandy *25*

Nigger *27*

Cygnus *29*

Bottle *30*

The Drowning Boy's Guide to Water *32*

Skin Theory *34*

Crepe Sole Shoes *36*

Iron Angel *40*

Oceans Are the Smallest Things *42*

Supernova *44*

Theater of America *46*

II

from The Bones We Lose *48*

III

The Black Boy's Guide to Blackness *56*

Memoir of a Plagiarist *57*

Smoke *58*

Between Skin *60*

Redwoods in the Hood *61*

Emmett Till Haunts the Library in Money, MS 64

No Flex Zone 65

Muriatic 67

Bishop on a Slant 69

Fresh Prince 72

Eulogy for the Confederate Battle Flag 75

Post-Racial America: A Pop Quiz 76

Reunion 79

Baby, ... 80

Solemn Pittsburgh Aubade 81

How to Heal a Boy's Fever 83

Firefly 84

Black Locusts 85

If a bag of silver coins and a bag of bullets sound the same 86

An Honest Prayer 88

Notes on Cameron Barnett 91

Acknowledgments 95

For Charlene, Michael, Dylan, and Afton.

I

WHEN THE MUTE SWANS RETURN

If you ask me, every spring should be spent
on the Seneca. The casual swirl
of wet fingers in the hard yawn of March,
knuckling your way through the cloudy slough;

your tousled likeness tonguing the surface,
the shape of you clapping in on itself,
everything slipping away in ripples.
What else would happen pulling at water?

When the mute swans return, a huff of leaves
escapes the nearby tree; the fledgling wind
refuses the home of your lungs. Only
the Finger Lakes catch its breath—a hiccup.

Sometimes the spring lakes feign themselves as clouds;
the mute swans—to fly—pull at the water.

NONBINDING LEGISLATION, OR A RESOLUTION

Whereas I'm as proud to be black as a tree is
to be made of wood. I've been black so long
I don't know what pride is anymore. I was told
it was a bad thing—I was told I should give it up
to the wind.

Whereas air blows hardest when you are nothing
more than the snap of a flag, a wind-whipped rolling
symbol. I am already a symbol—dark bark, sturdy.
Still I don't know what colors to hoist, what banner
belongs to me or how to hold it.

Whereas what I am has become cliché, roots
to canopy. Even this breath, my words
a post hoc paradigm hung out to dry,
and I feel flattest at the edges.

Whereas the race card is now everyone's card
in a deck I did not cut. I hate card games,
the conceit of the shuffle. I hate when white people
hate white people because hating white people
is fashionable. A person's color is a silly thing
to hate.

Whereas hate is a strong word
working out on every tongue red enough
to spew it or blue enough to covet it. Of this fixation
of color: a tree stripped of its bark is still a tree,
the hue of wood notwithstanding.

Whereas I don't understand why people are proud
on my behalf, their clench of flag and branch and the breeze
itself. How to be the tree in a forest you did not plant.
I have no other choice but to climb flagpole-high and wave
in this wind's song and dance.

Therefore be it resolved: I do not care
for my skin because it's always been
about my skin—but I have never been
about my skin. Not completely. Who is
this dying to wear my skin now?

TO THE OCTOPUS

I got coldcocked in the mouth once
        by a kid blacker than me for *Talking*
white to him outside the cafeteria,
        lost four teeth to the tiled hallway,

painted a stripe of red down my shirt.
        I'd speak of the pain, but I'm telling you
a story you already know. I have seen you
        cling to coral so tight you become every color

all at once. Camouflage is essential.
        We know this, but when I watch you
I realize how you can squeeze through
        most things if your mouth fits just right.

I'm still learning. I held half my mouth
        in a sandwich bag when my father picked me up
at school, couldn't tally each tooth
        in the blood-smeared plastic, asked me *What*

did you do? I'm trying to be more like you now.
        The other day I passed a brick wall, imagined
my arms fourfold, pressed my palms to it until
        there was no air, but I didn't turn tan. Later

I stood on a packed bus coiling my arms
        around the railing—still black. How do you shoot
skin out of your body? I've seen you leave
        limbs behind, each a little brain, distracting

predators. You think of anything to stay alive.
        I have to mind my mouth and limbs in public;

they don't grow back. My mother stayed
        in the operating room for hours. I was so

sedated she stayed by my side and never ate.
        I woke up to the dentist teasing her
about the churn in her stomach—*It was louder
        than my drill!* Mothers will starve for us,

they know this—hunger as second nature.
        Being eaten is what they call love, isn't it?
My gums leaked well into the summer. I stopped
        brushing for weeks, too many toothbrushes left

in peppermint swirl, my mouth unchanged
        save for the cursing of that kid's name.
Maybe if my blood were blue I'd have three hearts
        like you: one for forgiving, one for forgetting, one

for moving on. Watching you now I know why
        you blacken the water and run.

PURPLE RUCKLE

What tells the lemon to grow
       so curved in flavor? You cup
          the yellow of it like a
bubble bursting. I hold two more the same,
       each bruised from juggling.

It is sticky-hot inside.
       A passive breeze necks around
          the porch. The planks creak heavy
with afternoon. Mom lays out in short-shorts,
       says she is sick with

something only sunlight can
       cure. Her hands are tight as plum pits
          hanging at her side. We cut
a lemon and bite wedges, spit-sweet and
       tongue-callous. Through thick

rind the bruises taste bitter.
       Sour snickers between our
          teeth, puckered faces slowly
pulling apart from purple ruckle. Mom
       sleeps while she tans, burnt

till fever-red. You ask me
       to teach you juggling. I grab
          a new lemon; you wriggle
in, watch a small sunrise with every toss.
       Reverse cascade. Mom

twitches her fists in her sleep
        like a heartbeat. A lemon
                drops, more bruises. You ask me
how I learned to juggle. I say *Walking*
      with my hands open,

holding things with fingertips,
      and never squeezing too hard.
              More cascades, more bruises still.
Deep thuds stir Mom awake. She is sun-stenched,
      orange in the face.

You want to juggle lemons
      like me one day. I know that
            you aren't as young as I think
you are or want you to be. So we bite
      more wedges until

we're sour-cheeked and bitter green.
      In the next room Mom watches
            the TV through sand-bagged eyes,
glazed over when the weather report comes.
      Her body is stiff,

supine in the recliner,
      palms open—so deep and black
            and blue. We are prune-fingered
and yawning. All your eagerness, all this
      curiosity

like the tooth of a key deep
      inside you, tumbling. I have
            nothing to teach you—you
will learn the feeling of air through clenched nails,
      the weight of your wrists.

STACK

The half cord slumped in the backyard—I almost start
to say something. He knows firewood

heaped any which way doesn't burn well. *There's a lot
to read about woodpiles on the Internet,* Dad tells me.

The work gloves we've worn together since I was a boy—
once slack around my fingers, now my palms squeeze snug

into the leather. Lumber passed sideways. We talk with our eyes
to the ground, turning each log bark-side down. This keeps them

from soaking in too much water. So he says. The bark and I
share the same hue, I almost say. Spaces must be left

in the stacking for the wood to breathe. Winters have been warmer
for years. Sometimes I still struggle with the flue

and the smoke grows. Sometimes I don't lay the logs down
like he wants. Dad says, *You can tell a lot about a family*

by how it stacks its woodpile. When the rack is full, an old tarp
blown down the hill calls for a rope around a tree and me rappelling

through a thicket of dead leaves. I tie my waist and he holds
the neck of the line. I almost say something about childhood,

but when he starts to haul me up I realize I've grown
heavy in the mud beneath the leaves, and I pull.

We toss the tarp over the wooden row. *It's a matter of keeping in
as much as a matter of keeping out.* I only look at what we've built—

he kicks it, so we both know it's solid.

STEPPING INTO YOUR MOUTH

for Komunyakaa

The front door of anything is always a trap,
and so I have pried back your cellar doors,
the musk of mildew dank in the air like a breath
held long for something special, and I am almost certain
I'm stepping into your mouth—tell me what to do
with my shoes, which tooth to hang my coat on?
Epiglottis lamp chain, I yank light from your throat.
I am knocking over your furniture. I am not apologizing.
We are all guilty of something, and I am holding a fistful
of your cavities. Tell me what you love, and what
you regret. Your sofa's short arms and long spine call out
to me. I might stay awhile longer. I might pilfer
your sock drawer, empty your bathroom cabinets,
rearrange your spice rack, any little thing to move
your tongue. In a small vase you keep the seeds
of the Vietnam tree that stopped that bullet—the one
meant to shepherd you into that darkest cellar.
I put one seed in my pocket and tell myself
every adventure needs an amulet. I'm sure I will
find my way out of this house eventually, but not
tonight. I take another seed, place it in the palm
of your hand, ask you to write me a poem with it.
What did you lose in the war, and who was it meant for?
How do most men find death at the end of a gun barrel,
but you find poetry? I am full of more questions than you
can swallow. Now the tops of the windows bleed sunlight
above a curtain rod horizon, and I know it is only morning.
Yusef, it's going to be warm until November.
I might stay awhile longer.

COUNTRY GRAMMAR

My aunt no longer plants asparagus because *It attracts the worst kinds*
        of pests, she says, prostrate in the garden, tweezer fingers taut
around the necks of weeds, tidying the earth beside the parsley, chives,
        and rhubarb that grow strong stalks by her window. I spy

the lilacs, open the bags of soil we bought at the hardware store
        where two men stood behind us at checkout, bullhorns
for throats, calling each other *Nigger* as if it were the periods
        to their sentences. In the line I watched my aunt deliver

the kind of side-eye she saves for our folks, almost expect it when noon
        peers over our shoulders, the stiff scent of manure
everywhere. Side by side our knees dimple the dirt. She says *I don't know why*
        our people have to say that word everywhere we go—

I bury my nose in my shirt—*I don't care if it's n-i-g-g-a or n-i-g-g-e-r,*
        either way it makes me sick. She was my age when MLK
was shot. I try to ignore the rot in my hands. She is always focused
        on the dirt, so I turn my back to hide my eyes gazing at the hydrangeas.

I've never told her about Kyle in sixth grade who chanted *Nigger-nigger-*
        nigger at me every day during recess, and I'm not sure I could
justify why I never knocked knuckles through his braces, scared I'd strike
        something. I probably couldn't justify my love of Nelly then either,

rapping every word of "Country Grammar," the chest swell in my voice
        when I'd sing *Who say pretty boys can't be wild niggas?*—
how I didn't care which friends sang it with me, but only if we were singing.
        Even today, I couldn't justify when Malcolm introduced me

at the reading, called me *My nigga,* and whether or not I blushed I can't
        remember—but the clap of palms when we dapped, the cautious
laughter in the room, the smile I couldn't keep hidden, what is there
        to explain? I wonder how my aunt learned to love afternoons

back-bent in mud, to love the grime under her nails. *Good dirt,* she says,
        the key is good dirt. I bet those fools at the store don't know
how to grow a damn thing. I raise a dirty hand and touch the petals
        of a hibiscus—leave it smeared when I let go.

TRUE FACTS ABOUT WATER

I.
Ninety-four percent of life on earth
is aquatic. We all come from the ocean
at some point. The human womb
is a small ocean we all come from.
The body is built to be aquatic.

II.
Seventy percent of the planet is covered
in water, ninety-seven percent of which
is salty. Sunlight can only penetrate two hundred
meters into sea. The majority of the world
is in perpetual darkness.

III.
The first eyes evolved to see
through water. A human eye
is filled with it. There is no seeing
around it. There is no seeing
without it.

IV.
We boil water to get rid of impurities.
"Impurity": anything of color you can see in the water—
anything in the water you can't see.

V.
Eight glasses a day is a myth. The body speaks
of hydration through thirst, which is to say
you only need as much water as your body requests.

VI.
When I see a black body I am reminded of water:
pools, rivers, drinking fountains, triangle trade—
always a removal, a taking away, taking out, taken from.

VII.

Earth is a closed system; the water of today is the water
of a billion years ago, and a billion years hence.

VIII.

"Hyponatremia": intoxication by water.
Running.
Caused by too much water in the body.
Filling.
Most likely to happen during bouts of intense athletic activity.
Fatal.

IX.

Humans can only use about three-tenths of all the water on earth.

X.

"Watercolor": pigment suspended in solution.

XI.

In developing nations, women are responsible for collecting water.
In every nation, men are responsible for wasting it.

XII.

The human body is composed
of up to sixty percent water; the brain
and heart seventy-three percent;
the lungs eighty-three percent, bones
thirty-one percent. Water helps
the body digest, flush waste and toxins,
regulate temperature, deliver
oxygen, protect the brain and spine
from shock.

XIII.
The properties of water are essential
to life, and also strange: osmosis,
the Mpemba effect, bending light
into distortion. By nature, water is polarized—
by nature, bodies are always distorted,
are always picking sides.

XIV.
Surface tension is what kills you when you hit water too hard.

LETTER TO SANDY

I know it must have been hard for you, Mrs. K,
   the morning you told your daughter to choose
between her black boyfriend and your family.

   It must have been tough to find the right words
in all those tears. Water can be so difficult sometimes.
   A good mother never wants her child to hurt,

after all, but pain is more than feeling. I know it.
   I can hear it in the metallic tinging
of silverware set on the kitchen table before my mom

   places a large pot of pasta on the trivet. At twelve
I slipped a steak knife from the drawer and cut up my hands
   and arms at the table, so sure there was good white skin

beneath the black. I wanted to look like the other kids at school.
   I remember the splat of a rock dropped into silt,
the quick hush of a wave licking up more silt to bury the rock.

   It drowned out everything. A year later I was standing
in the Sunglass Hut and wanted to be invisible. I'm sure you know
   the clerk's pain, Mrs. K, as she watched me move

between display cases and thought my fingers were lock picks
   laid on the glass, her vigilance hair-triggered and happy,
the sound of her voice when she whispered into the phone,

   the footsteps of the security guard and his voice: *Son,
you're gonna have to find a new store.* Where would you go
   if you couldn't go anywhere? You should know

how I begged my dad not to go back into the store after I told him,
   that my begging might have saved the clerk's life, might
have saved his. You and I know how to choke back tears, Sandy.

But I know the things you wanted me to be because I wanted them
long before you did. Hush—it's okay. I know how pain sounds
in a mother's voice. That sink of sand into lungs—I know that, too.

NIGGER

It's the way your second *G* catches
                in my throat that feels
        most like drowning.
                It's the way your hard *R*
                      drips over my lips,

        and I am told, even though
I am black, that we do not talk about you.
        It's the way I don't even know
                who you are that makes this moratorium

                so absurd.
Are you African or American
      or both
              or neither? Sable child
         swathed in mystery, scimitar-swift,

            and lithe-hearted—what do you stand for?
     Time is a great veil, and I am asking you
to pull it aside and speak. I know
      of your kings and their kingdoms,
           of your daughters and sons

        shipped between sail and sea salt,
    a pythagorean pattern of profit. So tell me how much
more than this you are.
     I want your truth, your thinkers, your music,
        the rhythms of your blood,

     its beating. Name this for me. Call this something
more than ancestry. Call your people
      the first humans. Speak up.
            Why do you mumble
your lineage? You shift like a shadow

seeking itself while hiding
            from moonlight. Are you a shapeshifter,
      limb-lugged, body limp
in the tree of Truth, melancholy melanin
            face flecked with tears?

                  Then I will weep with you. I will cry
for the thieved and trafficked,
                        the pummeled and punctured.
            I will cry for the harnessed, the hated,
      the hunted; the can't-votes, the can't-works, the can't-

                        rides, the can't-earns, the can't-lives;
for the lynched,
            and all the fire thrown at you.
      I will cry for this
hand-me-down history,

                  for your native tongues
            lost in the melting pot, the ink of heritage
      wet on the page and vanishing. Who are you? A six-letter slur
            slunk deep beneath our tongues
or six letters strong?

      Who are you, nigger? African beauty
            behind American façade. You were not born
      from a womb of nooses. You need not hang
your head in a new world.

CYGNUS

What is the opposite of water?
     a skeleton frowning,
     three femurs in a ditch,
     a honeycomb filling the
     gooey heart-hole, spilling
What is the opposite of a parade?
     a familiar voice, thundercracked
     across the sky; a crow's tongue
     split in two, the crow speaking
     short stabbing sentences, making
What is the opposite of a guess?
     love in the form of a mistake,
     me and you in the form of
     Cygnus in July—or perhaps
     Draco, but there seems to be
What is the opposite of a constellation?
     a quorum of light receding
     from where we are to where
     we came from—two mirrors
     facing each other, shattered.

BOTTLE

The slow silhouette of your pouring is thin
against the wall, and for that I thank you.

I'm walking, floorboards like piano keys, but the air
in the room is just air. The yawn of the glass looms rouge.

I have never been in a mouth so big. Hello, pinot. Hello,
cork dust. Hello, sulfites. You have a way of making

each second feel like two, and tonight is a good night
for ghost stories. The label goes dark. Your neck goes dark.

Wide lips are tinted. When I put your mouth to my ear it's the throat
of the ocean that's the loudest. I will see dead children crawling

up the walls if that's what you want, but don't let them laugh. Goodbye,
pillow. Goodbye, shut eye. Goodbye, nighttime. Thank you for the red

mouth, for complicating my relationship to sweet things. Because
of this, the muscle beneath my teeth is learning to quick twitch.

You have a way of making a voice box a container, and this makes me
want to be an archivist. I read about a pillar in Hamburg, Germany,

that the whole town signed and then buried. This can be our little secret:
my spine sinking beneath my skin into your gravity. You are too good

not to remind me we have already been here. I swear last January
was two years ago, but you have a way of shrinking the universe.

Under these stars, the oldest light we can see is a small patch of red.
How familiar. I imagine when **God** decided to start the cosmic stopwatch

he must have been thinking about a sunset, its lowest streaks, the winking
hue of the horizon. I see it when you kiss me. Before I say *I love you*

I want to burn my tongue on your tongue, learn a language nobody knows.
They say the moon pulls the tides over the planet, so I must be the

the drunkest thing beneath the sea. Hello, smooth sip. Hello, big pour.
Hello, hollow. I like the way you are a lighthouse—

because I know how to drown
I'm not afraid to get wet.

THE DROWNING BOY'S GUIDE TO WATER

Remember, the strength of chlorine,
       the indoor pool, swim class clinging
to the kickboard then jumping from the ledge
       into the arms of the smiling white lady,
only mostly sure she would catch you,
       Mom calling *Cameron! Cameron!*
to get you to look, then said *Kick, kick!* Remember,
       there's nothing a mother won't do
for one still shot of your head
       above the water. It's important
to always practice good form: kick your legs. Remember
       Tortola, the sea like melted marbles and the sun
at the equator, your brown skin browning; with a stretch
       of snorkel between your teeth you jumped in
and chased a sea turtle for the length
       of the tiny island's beach, the pressure
in your ears right when you thought you could catch it,
       Mom and Dad sighing when you came back
to the surface. Remember your worst fear
       is not being able to breathe. Most people who drown
are brown, and eighty percent of people who drown
       are male. Don't forget to kick your legs.
Don't forget middle school musicals, all the costumes
       and makeup, the white boys making jokes
about blackface, the laughter gurgling in their necks,
       no one else like you to back you up.
Sometimes you will swallow water. Remember, a throat
       is the size of a Skittle or a hole in a hoodie,
and Trayvon's legs kicked hard against the night. Drowning
       isn't loud or splashy, it's silent—autonomic,
neck tilt, and terror. When you are drowning, feet become rocks,
       hands push down water in vain, and the thump

of blood is the only thing that can be heard. It is all, supposedly,
        painless. Always remember that. Always remember
your first girlfriend's grandmother sneering at the sight
        of her white arms wrapped up in your hoodie,
how you pretended it was painless, but you couldn't
        help but *Kick your legs*; or how nobody
will save you anymore when you yell *I can't breathe*
        so just *Kick your legs*; or every sidewalk
where a white girl sees you, pulls her phone up to her face,
        and crosses the street like she's guarding
something secret—*Kick your legs*; remember that you have been
        a white girl's secret before—*Kick your legs*.
When you are drowning, don't forget to practice good form:
        float on the surface; part the water with your lips;
only swallow as much as you can hold.

SKIN THEORY

A crookedness laid bare
        around me. I want to find where
the water breaks through.
            A finger pointed
        to all the wrong places—this is the first discovery.

                Consider the weight of hypothesis,
     evaporated.
         And where have all the alchemists gone?
An idea
        transmitted through air.
             I can't recall when it was
I asked for your thoughts on a rare disease.
           The report: itchy cuticles.
     The evidence: cold flesh in a bottle,
          a bunsen burner set low,
sweat as approximate calculation.

     Then came the shedding,
a brief lull of light
        lipped into the eyes. A slow gripping.
           The word "vessel" scrawled somewhere.
             Here are your methods. How to translate them.
How the throat becomes
        a tin can telephone stretched
          from space to space.

     I called you with the intent of silence.

                So much has been broken
        on the surface. Watch the meniscus
    drown. Watch the leather learn
           where to buckle and breathe.

I want you to believe, to say the word
         "proof" with me. Yes, this is
                  a fragile thing. So much can change—
                           never just black and white
layers.

         In the end,
all I can give you is some small
         clasp of skin, the wrinkled space
our chemistry has left behind.

CREPE SOLE SHOES

I.
You were anchored fast
by the cotton gin fan
pinning your head in shoal.
Barbed wire plaited around
your collar. Tell me how still
the water was—squashed
bullfrog for a face. Did the fish
notice you? Did they nuzzle
your cheeks? Or scatter?
Tell me how the river broke
around your bloated body, for days.
Tell me where it was deepest.

II.
How many buttons
were on Mrs. Bryant's
dress? Tell me how it
clung to her behind
the register. Were you
really so cocky? What
did you say to her?
Did you make eyes
at her—skin the color
of cracked pearls—
call her *Baby*? Why?
Tell me it isn't true.
You didn't sass her.
It was Mississippi
and you were just
a nigger
buying gum.

III.
When was the last time
Mamie ever called you
Bo? Fourteen years old.
Today, you could
be my grandfather.
I want to put you
back together, but
how can I rebuild
you? In Chicago
you left your watch,
took your father's ring
and the train to Money.
That summer of '55
the rails beneath you
steadily pinned down
the Illinois horizon.
Were you ever afraid?

IV.
Bryant and Milam wrapped
their trial tongues in stars and bars.
Old Uncle Mose pointed a finger
as tired and strong as
every southern black.
In the jury room
white men laughed
and drank pop to stall—
just enough to look good.
Months later, $4,000
and a confession.
Damn if that nigger
didn't have Crepe Sole shoes.
You know how hard they are to burn?

V.
Was Orion watching
down from the sky,
or Libra, the night
they snatched you?
Who did you miss most
when they took you
to their shed? You
were tied up like meat,
hands numb up to the wrists
while they took turns
smashing your face.
He chopped your nose
with the pistol butt,
crammed his fingers in
your socket, pulled your eye
out, down to your cheek,
rested, then threw you back
into the truck. They Picasso'd
your face. Took it to the backwoods,
that hillside slope. How do you
scream when no one cares?

VI.
Muddy water caught the bullet
spilling out from your head.
Your corpse broke the Tallahatchie
waves. And splashing, you
sparked a powder keg
of negroes, who marched well
after your lungs became thermoses
clod with Mississippi's shame.
When your picture hit

the newspapers, even white
America doubled-over
and groaned.

VII.
They say your whistle
curdles the wind in
Montgomery. They say
the sidewalks were heavy
with your footsteps in Selma.
They say after a storm
in Money, the ground
turns pink in memory
of you.

IRON ANGEL

Freedom Corner. My knees kiss concrete. Dirt is the first sign
of forgetting. The leaves that accompany it—deciduous flair,

red crinkles and orange flakes, a finely ground autumn snow
blown into cracks in the wall beneath the iron body. Every inch

of the ground feels like braille. I find my grandfather's name
embossed in the granite, Centre and Crawford. This is the biggest circle

in the city that has been forgotten. Even the dirt has grown gray, caked up
in the crevices of a hundred names. An empty Cheetos bag in the wind

drags over the name Alma Speed Fox. I met her on Saturday, and now
I am clearing her name on Sunday. She is my grandfather's neighbor,

Bishop Foggie. There is a cigarette butt tucked in the trunk of the *F*.
I flick it toward a pigeon cowered under a broken old TV monitor

that I can only assume used to play some informative video. The tape still
stuck inside it, I'm sure, must be dust by now. Dust is the only thing

that hasn't forgotten this place. In the granite wall, an iron body dreams
its arms are wings, head up to the sky, looking over the corner. I imagine

it's a woman. I imagine she is Freedom. I imagine the patina tailing down
her sliver of torso is partly tears. I can see the water flowing, splashing

deep into the granite, digging a small pool in the rock over time, unwatched
and unkempt. And in the winter the freezing pool must expand

and contract, a sort of breathing, a sort of release. New paths are made
from cracking open old barriers. Beneath this woman, this angel, this iron

African, there must be an aquifer seeded with her weeping. The dust
of Pop's name, of the other hundred names, must blow its way in,

must mingle into a sediment or a sludge, carve its way through the
underground, churning in the belly of the city like something not quite

fully digested, or maybe pooling somewhere, swelling. I look toward
the Point, its fountain at full blast—a circle the city cannot ignore.

OCEANS ARE THE SMALLEST THINGS
for A

In high school I could name all the flags of the world, could
        rap projects for English class, could hustle the basketball
court, scraping up my hands, heels, knees, knuckles, and elbows,
        but I couldn't keep my friend from cutting herself
when no one was watching. No arms or legs, nothing

        that would show. A said she didn't want to be *One of those*
freaks, but the hiss of the blade over the skin of her ribs
        was a welcomed distraction. I had to hold her
gently or sometimes not at all. In biology they taught us
        how deep the sea was, how we didn't know everything

that lived down deep, but what I really needed to know was how
        to make a hug hurt less, or what to say on AIM
when A told me she was raped by someone she knew,
        started to tell me by saying: *Cam, I think I did a bad thing.*
A, who loved the color orange. A, who sang opera, a wrestler

        who quoted *The Breakfast Club* constantly, who played
clarinet and always found reasons to laugh about anything.
        She traded shirts in shades from apricot to pumpkin for hoodies
gray as pencil lead and hid her head, arms crossed, tears on desks
        building up like oceans. How to navigate this. How to comfort

the victim when her best friends blamed her. How to confront
        her attacker the day he stood twenty lockers down from us,
his sneer wide as the hallway, hands pocketed, a bell separating me
        and him between fifth period and a brawl, A shaking behind me,
eyes submerged in my shoulder, water rising. To make myself a wall

        or a tsunami. How to destroy him or be destroyed
before he ever touched a single cell of hers again. They didn't teach me
        how to help her find her laughter when it was lost, to share

my dreams with her so that her nights could be full of something
        other than darkness. Even though I knew faith was a muscle

in each of us, how long it took to flex. How long before she could look me
        or anyone in the eye for more than a moment. How long
before even I could touch a woman and not fear him. Some things you have
        to learn for yourself. There's a reason we'll never again walk
the front steps of our high school, where the busses waited after wrestling

        matches, where A waited alone for a ride home. Sometimes
you don't get to choose where scars surface. We caught up years later.
        She showed me photos of her children while I stared
at the ring on her finger, swinging at her side as we walked the edge
        of my college campus overlooking the county jail, and I swore

I saw her attacker press his face in every cell window. A couldn't look
        so she imagined taking the prison apart brick by brick
and stacking each one on his chest one at a time until he knew the pressure,
        knew it could kill him. Some things you have to learn
for yourself. I mentioned the river churning behind the jail seemed a

        better place to put him, that it flowed to bigger rivers
and those flowed out to the ocean. I'll never forget she said: *Oceans are*
        the smallest things. I'll never forget that day, how when I moved
to hug her goodbye we both flinched.

SUPERNOVA

The little boy I babysit loves Hot Wheels and Zoids,
        keeps a dusty Nerf gun under his bed. He prefers K'NEX
                to LEGOs, has knobby knees and gapped teeth,
red-brown skin like me. In his room there's a telescope by the window

        where his brother's bed used to be. At night we sit there,
necks bent, eyes to the glass. He just started fifth grade,
        so there's a star in the galaxy for every question
            he asks me: *Was the Big Bang real? Are aliens real?*

When they die do they go to heaven too?
        I want to tell him about the other side
of the universe where bombs go off that we never know about
        for millennia. I've learned to boil answers down to one word—*Yes.*

                Maybe. Hopefully. I've learned one word is all it takes
to break a kid—only ten, but he leaves rooms when he hears black
        boy's names on the news. He gets quiet when guns go off
in movies, so I turn the TV off at night. We don't say his brother's name.

        On the couch he finds more questions. *How do stars stay*
            in the sky? I say *Gravity,* want to say *I don't know*
how to explain, say *But you can recognize it by how the planets fall*
        toward them, say *Everything out there is always falling.*

He falls asleep with his feet against my thigh, kicks them
        when he's dreaming, and I want to kiss his forehead, want
            to calm him. He reminds me how close we are
to explosion, that things always break apart from the center.

        He's lived it—a kid who loves space. He teaches me things, too:
In 50,000 years the Little Dipper will shift, will resemble more of a bent,

crushed Coke can, the hind leg of Ursa Minor collapsing into its gut.
I'm afraid he will become like the stars of Draco,

serpentine curve twisted into shipwreck. He deserves more than this—
a solar system spinning around him, every scrap of gravity left over
from the Big Bang. I want to take the boiling stone from his core, name it
Dignity, mold it while hot, christen it with a kiss and cool it

into something the world will recognize, but I don't want
to betray him. How many stars named after black kids or light-years until
the next supernova? I want him to know what room America has left
for black love, black boys, black families. Maybe. Hopefully.

One night I dreamt Emmett Till visited Ferguson, Missouri.
Nobody recognized him. Not until he laid down
next to Michael Brown's body. Not until he kissed him.

THEATER OF AMERICA

for Michael Brown

"The one in front of the gun
lives forever." —Kendrick Lamar

I want to let the silence of snow melt into you. I want
to take your name and skywrite it in permanent marker
then let the rain tattoo you everywhere. This is what to do
with black bodies. In the theater of America fire sprinklers
cover everything in shallow pools. I want to give you
a monsoon instead—it's the safest waters where most drown.

In the theater of America there are none so blind
as those who will not see color. They fill the aisles,
tongues wrapped in Gadsden flags. This is what they do
with black bodies: fill them with lead, let them fall,
let them sink, let them float in thin puddles. Even if
I could crush this theater inside my fist, I would
feel the small hammering of people rebuilding already.

And what is left of you? What about black bodies?
Your home is the rock of Sisyphus; your story is a book
the blinded are placing on a shelf in a library they have
never been to; yours is the prodigal play in which black
sons do not return home. Your body rests on the apron
of the stage. And somewhere in the mezzanine I hear a whisper
sailing like fishing line over still water: *Blackness is always*
knowing where you are, but never knowing where you're from.
And from the rafters an echo: *Blackness is always knowing*
...never knowing.

II

from **THE BONES WE LOSE**

I. The Note Broker

His eyes are the color of cracked crayons
rubbed end to end. In the alleyway he lies
way down, thinner than a nine-cent dime.
His hand catches the slick of a magazine,
pulls it up hoping for sheet music. Instead
he reads about the pieces that were cut
from the Shroud of Turin. His hands hold
crumpled corners of pages, fingers dotted
long ago with paper cuts from a love letter.
A bone inside a bone is breaking. There are
small memories at work between thumb
and forefinger. He knows the more a thing
is understood, the more it is destroyed.

In the distance a trumpet blares
asthmatically, his blood crooning
around each failed note. Beyond
the brick wall, people are talking—
the type who speak only from the neck.
The type who don't know a song
from an echo. But the words inside him
are not these. The chip on his shoulder
is made of sawdust. Their song is not
his, which is to say every rib in his body
is a tuning fork waiting to be struck.

II. The Accomplice

None other than the Bishop of Blues, aka Hank the Hotstepper,
        Godfather of Brass and Barbells, flexing that sharkskin
double-breasted suit with matching trumpet case. It's no wonder

he rolls into town on white-wall tires with more pep than
        seventy-six trombones in the morning sun. Manhole covers rattle
like snake tails, and spit sewer steam on his black suede shoes.

With nothing but a shrug and a swagger-step he brings out sinners
        in a septic city, shaking tempest-hard, and for a time people
are weak-kneed, wailing like ten-foot tubas. When he enters The Omni

he casts a wily wink toward Karma, orders an Old Fashioned, and sips
        real smooth. Never mind her kiss clotting in his heart—a black
spot sinking in like a splinter—or the Jankowski men high and tight

on his neck where his close shave stops. The thick sheen of an ax handle
        flashes in his eyes. Could have seen it coming. He's at the coat check
whistling "Sweet Home Chicago," and no one speaks while the mob moves

outside like a rugby scrum backlit in scarlet—the Hotstepper's teeth filling
        the cold cracks in cobblestone, a pale horse clip-clops the street,
while inside a high note hits the air, ringing like a syllable for revenge.

III. The Son

Fumbling down to the corner of Fifth and Liberty, his tongue
plays mute to the trumpet of his throat. When he goes to sing
"Minnie the Moocher" the notes on sheet music clump into braille.
His pockets are lined with his father's old business cards—
papier-mâché in his palms. He holds memory like a walking stick
whittled into a spear. Fingers blistered from pay phone slots,
he's never held anything sharper than his father's tongue.

Heat lightning smacks the evening sky. At Joe's he greets the bartender
with a bar code tattooed on her neck. He asks to know what it says,
mouth like a bus at midday on Forbes Avenue. She says it's her name—
riot-eyed, he watches her lips move like an old Betty Boop rotoscoped
around a homonym for pleasure. His heart jellyfishes in his chest,
lust-blooded. He wants her taste in the back of his throat, wants the wet
of his tongue to scan her, knows how much is hidden between the lines.

Outside the bar, the road is steel scrap-black from rain—flecks of gold
hugging the tops of warming lampposts. The grandeur of the courthouse
falls against streets he has combed for change. He hears his mother's voice
ping like a coin flip ringing in the skull: *Not every penny facing heads-up
is worth grabbing.* On Centre Avenue he watches a spider spin a web
in the crook of a stop sign—notices how the web is just a history
of where the spider has been. He pokes his finger into it and admires
how far the thread will pull without breaking.

IV. The Wife

The house no longer has any music to it, so she hums
       what she thinks is "The Blue Danube"
and stirs her husband's broken violin in bathwater.
       It's the only one left. Sitting thigh-flat
on wet bathroom tile, the wall is thick with his smell—
       she peels off its paint chips, pressing fingertips
into plaster underbelly till they sting down to the quick.
       Twenty violins will keep the lights on
she tells herself. For days she has been soaking the violin
       from scroll to chin rest, believing the broth
will bring back the family business, knowing anything
       will come apart if stirred enough.

On the third day the resin begins to fail. Late September
       sunlight floods the backyard shed
where the band saw's shadow leans like a gramophone bell.
       Behind heavy machinery, boxes of horse hair
litter her husband's old workspace, pieces of woodwinds
       and loose reeds, lacquer and varnish
left behind. When she thinks of him working there, his back
       to her like a waning moon, the blood returns
to her nail beds. *How simple it was for him,* she thinks, holding
       necks of violins in ways he never held her.
She takes the soaked one, pulls apart the wood and strings
       till she learns its anatomy, and starts to build.
She makes twenty in an afternoon—each worse than the last.
       When she casts a defeated glare back
to the first one from the tub, only then does she see its flaws:
       warped fingerboard, crooked belly,
a bridge collapsed by the taut of the strings. Only then
       does she remember how the music
in the house scraped like train wheels down long tracks.

In the evening, she pulls out the box of their old love letters,
       tugging the first one she ever wrote him

from the tight stack. She reads a long forgotten story she
        told him—how as a child, she was surprised
that a person could "sew a dress." She thought it meant a person
        could do it by sewing alone, sewing one thread
onto another.

V. The Note Broker

There is snow on everything
        he has left behind. He watches
                icicles hang from awnings like dead men.

His lips mumble the fourth
        movement of *Scheherazade*. Help
                is too far away. He's in the deep of the alleyway

looking for her, the way a fish
        pokes its face through water. No light
                finds its way here in December. When he flips

his wrists over, shaking harder
        than a conductor's baton, the needle tip
                sinks mosquito-soft into his skin. Prayers fall flat

from folded hands, blood-threaded,
        while his fingertips slip on the lip of a dumpster.
                In his heart's fun house he kaleidoscopes himself,

watching with a gaze that could turn spheres
        inside out. He recites the words for love
                in all the languages he remembers, lets them swing

over his tongue the way hope sways inside us
        like a pendulum. He knows how a collarbone can feel
                like the slack of a noose waiting to snap.

THE BLACK BOY'S GUIDE TO BLACKNESS

In this town, rock salt purples the snow;
cold air too thick to see each other
downtown, amid the poor and busy
following the purple to avoid
stepping on toes. Elsewhere, an army

widow lights a cigarette, watches
the snowman in her yard begin to
melt. In her hands, a box full of her
husband's letters. Another puff—soon
the box will be bursting with ashes.

At the high school, a black boy thumbs through
an old copy of August Wilson's
Fences. He feels the spotlight coming
when the teacher asks the class to read
parts—no one likes to say the word, but

all want to hear it. At the bookstore,
a skeptic buys a bible before close.
He takes his purchase to the corner
of the café and he reads, surprised
at how small and many the words are.

In this snow-strapped town, the raw air grinds
with gritting teeth. Purple-footed folk
breathe hard and step carefully on by.
The cross-eyed bible reader squints for
the truth. A widow turns to ash all

that had been steel in her. In this town,
the black boy stands before his class, says
Nigger right into their eyes, then sits.

MEMOIR OF A PLAGIARIST

I wrote *Hamlet* in a summer, *Moby Dick* in a year, mastered loss,
and penned "Prufrock" on a rainy day. My love told me stories
were just masks of words, all guise no guts. Once I conquered literature

I moved to music: "Auld Lang Syne" and "Amazing Grace," "The Star-
Spangled Banner" for starters. Sometimes I didn't know my next song
until somebody sang it first—but I wrote it, lyrics like a signature

everyone recognized but nobody knew was mine. My love told me
songs were just earrings. When they no longer sufficed I moved on
to building, stacked silver to the sky and called it *Chrysler*, built

a bridge so strong my lover named it *Brooklyn*—each time I carved
my name in the nooks where no one noticed. I learned so many things
could be secrets, but my love told me a secret is just the valley

between a truth and a lie. Soon building was easy, so I started stealing
light everywhere it fell, balled it up, hurled into the night and made Aries,
Aquarius, Pegasus, Pisces, the Pleiades. I slept at my love's side,

crescent clutch under the sky I'd sewn. When she told me the people
in her dreams were made of clay I didn't believe her, so I became a dream,
rewired neurons until her nights were a seamless cinema. But I forgot

a perfect story isn't perfect until it finds its flaw. My love forgot me—
I became a thin sliver in her mind, more waning than waxing;
a needle threading itself to light, unlooping every time.

SMOKE

When my uncle fought fire he didn't use a hose
like his father before him—he used a straw
to sip orange juice and watched the sun flicker
between the curtains each morning. He fought
fire all his life in the hospital, though bedridden.
Dad used to tell me *He has a hard time with things
the rest of us do everyday.* I never did meet him,
but I knew his good and bad days by my aunt's
crow's feet or how Dad's knuckles rolled under his skin
when they came home from visits and played Art
Blakey in the living room so loud I couldn't hear
them talk, I never questioned why
I couldn't see him. I never asked if I could.

In a hospital I pass often, my uncle scales a ladder
and leaps through flames, taking an ax to every locked door.
I don't yet know that the house is him, that something keeps
rekindling the fire every time he puts it out. If one can say
a house is the space just above your throat, the whole thing
furnished basement to attic and burning, I can imagine
my uncle leaning deep in his rocking chair, embers spread
around him in a big lagoon, the pick of his ax-head blunted,
kissing his heel as it slides from his lap, and just outside the window
his brother and sister waving their bodies wildly to fight
the fire too, and that after a lifetime it might be hard
not to see them as candles.

My aunt tells me he saw my graduation pictures once and gave
something that looked like a smile. I learn where the thyroid is
when cancer comes for his neck and threatens to finish
where the flames are failing. In the end, it's not the fire that kills.

Once in a while I'll walk home and look up to see smoke
coming from the next neighborhood over and I wonder
if I might be watching someone's death not too far from me.
It happens most often in spring right before it rains
and the smell of what's lost falls all afternoon.

I turned down giving my uncle's eulogy
because they buried him in a jar
and I didn't know the right words
to make a good first impression.

Tonight I'm writing you a letter, Bruce, though it's winter now
and Dad is filling the fireplace with logs from the woodpile
even though the chimney may be too cold for the smoke to rise.

BETWEEN SKIN

Suppose I say the word "autumn," and write
"satchel" on a small blank notecard, lick it
closed in an envelope and mail it to you
so as you open it, standing alone in your cold
kitchen, you recall crimson leaves crunching

under our feet, the smell of the steep city trail,
how we split clammy palms long enough
for a love note to slip beneath the red-patched flap
of your bag, the corners of your grin pinned back
with hesitation, our shoes kicking up the dirt.
Or would you remember one evening that winter:

over heated pots, your mother's steady stirring;
bag in hand, the draw of your wrist unzipping,
my notes pouring onto the table, the pinch of
sleeve and skin in the zipper teeth, your mother's
sparrow-eye catching you flush-faced, the sigh
and swift spurn of her snatching the red leather?

I know I am hard to remember sometimes,
especially when the morning finds you
only mostly clothed, blushing by the sink
with your coffee and a simple card reading
"satchel." Just think of it as a missed kiss,
and that sting at the wrist, the tug between skin
and bone is the way I remember you, too.

REDWOODS IN THE HOOD

I.
If I said *Ghost Story* would you think of the woods?
Campfire busy with crackling, a standard jet-black night
behind a huddle of people, one of them telling some impossible story,
the rest leaning in, jumping with every pop of flame on a log?

If I said *Ghost Story* would you think of a casket?
The inside of a black church, busy with pictures of the
deceased, a mother-father-sister-brother-aunt-uncle stepping up
to the pulpit having to tell the impossible story, their ears still
attuned to the pop of a pistol, bodies felled from the weight of it all?

II.
Did you know that trees communicate with each other? Did you know
that fungus is the Internet of the forest? Did you know a mother tree
can send its children nutrients through the fungi? Did you know you pass
through a living room of laughter when you walk through the park?

III.
Walking in the park with my love I decide to name all the fallen trees
after black bodies: Renisha, Philando, Rekia, Alton. She is quiet.
The woods are hushed. A branch clatters under the weight of a bird.

IV.
In my poetry class I tell a group of 7th graders that a good way to learn
about metaphors is to think about trees. *What are all the parts of a tree?*
What have you seen trees do? What do they look like? Use all those
descriptions as metaphors. The kids stare at me. *I love using trees,*
I laugh—the kind of laugh that says I know I'm not serious but yes I am
serious and they should take me seriously too. We start working.
The paper they write on is thin, and it tears as they erase.

V.
If I said the word "deciduous" would you think of autumn
and spiced coffees, gourds and ghouls on every doorstep,
a rake plowing through a yard of leaves piling up and up and up?

If I said *Deciduous* would you think of little boys
with dark faces and little girls with dark faces and continue to
rake them up into piles, bag them, and leave them to be taken?

VI.
We only think a tree is dead if it has fallen, but the forest knows
long before then. We relish in watching the fall, then squirm at the rot.
We never stick around to see everything in it eventually come back
to the living.

VII.
In another class I tell a group of 5th graders to imagine
impossible things and write about how they came to be.
What is the other side of the moon hiding? I ask, *What
do the grass and stones say to each other? What do trees
dream about?*

VIII.
Dreams of rain, dreams of seeds,
dreams of petals and pulse, dreams
of forests breathing, dreams of me—
bark and branch, dreams from my roots,
dreams from the other side of the woods,
dreams from my father, dreams from my mother,
dreams from the atmosphere, dreams from
mountaintops, dreams from tomorrow,
dreams from yesterday, dreams of prosperity,
dreams of survival, dreams without end.

IX.

If I said the word "evergreen" would you plant one?
If I told you to plant an evergreen tree where would you dig?
If I helped you dig, can you promise not to come back cutting?
Can a forest be more than just for reaping?
Can a tree's roots be more than lips
searching in the deep, dark dirt?
Is a black kid allowed to be
more than a ghost story
waiting to be told?

X.

As much as one could say a black body is a tree, one could say
this planet has more forests than we ever thought. And if black
bodies can be any tree, let them be redwoods, let them grow strong
and sturdy, let them have crowns unparalleled, let them stand
a millennium, let them be *Ambassadors from another time*, let them be
plentiful and prospering, let them be, let them be, let them...

XI.

I didn't grow up in the hood, but my backyard is the edge
of a forest. If a tree falls in the woods and no one is there
to see it, who can say whether its life mattered or not?

EMMETT TILL HAUNTS THE LIBRARY IN MONEY, MS

What I can't let you know is that death, too, is a snore,
a sooty shelf of unmoving paper with some gasbag
lady at the front desk. If you knew, there'd be too many
questions about how I sneak past heaven's gates some days
to nap against the silent stacks, feel the blood in my head
drip into the young adult fiction. Mamie always preached

good posture, so I sit straight at least. When I was black
I grew used to the shuffle of visibility, to the *Move boy!* and
the thousand yard stare over my head. Being ghost
isn't all new or scary—no one to ask me what came out
of my lips sixty years ago. I might as well be ink
on closed pages, lost somewhere in the archives. You can't judge

a book by its facts or flaps or back cover, but a black boy
is the title and the illustration staring you in the face, asking
to be seen or sampled but not smothered between the other
black boys, forgotten, dog-eared, and ditched. I don't love death,
but I don't mind reading the periodicals for faces like mine,
putting names to the ones I'll welcome through the gates soon.

NO FLEX ZONE

Zone of swag.
Zone of Swae and Slim.
Zone of *Balmain zippers*.
Zone of fast money and fast cars
pulling up in slow neighborhoods.
Zone of no neighborhood. Zone of boys meandering
in vacant streets. Zone of no responsibilities.
Zone of force field, shielding my steez
from your flex. Zone for accept it—don't think.

Zone of blind.
Zone of hungry.
Zone where boy rides a skateboard with rope
in hand from the back of a car. Where boy rides
outside the zone. Zone growing. Zone of peers
regurgitating words for fame and success
and come up and made it. Zone of slaves.
Zone of cakewalk. Zone of zombie-walk,
of small steps, of deadness. Zone of the dead,
of the landfill, of broken art and broken culture.
Zone of lost culture. Zone of no culture.

Zone of false wealth. Zone of grin
and fake and front and flex.
Zone of *Gold fangs*, of *Gold chains*, of no games.
Zone not-for-you. Not your flex.
Zone of look at me. Of looking at you
looking at me. Of me mocking the way
you look. Zone of get-your-own. This is my
sound; your sound lies beyond this zone.
Zone so empty, ear drums bend from the slightest
noise. The least of music. The thinnest words.

Zone where: *H2O, lean—same thing.*
Zone of poison. Zone of empty thoughts.
Zone of thots. Zone of women dancing
for paychecks—women boys don't
really care about. Zone of crooked ethos.
Zone of flat thoughts and flat words.
Zone for the same uninspired dancing from the same
uninspired dancers. Zone of no original thots.
Zone of bros before hoes. Zone of drought.
Zone where lips love spliff and purp and sizzurp more
than their women. Zone where no one minds. No one
talks about it, because why? *All my hoes, they so rude.*

Zone of poverty. Zone of short term.
Zone of *Mike Will Made It* and so can I.
Zone of boy posing as Kool Moe Dee. Flexing.
Trill-ass individual. Zone of name-drop.
Zone of see me, hate me, love me, respect me.
Zone of nothing. Zone of hypocrisy.
Zone of lost boys rolling nowhere
real slow—monkey see, monkey do.
Zone of reflex. Of spasm coming from the gut,
of uncontrolled sameness. Zone of black hole.

Zone we have fallen into. Zone one foot in the grave.
The other foot tapping its way closer. Zone of dirt.
Zone of deflect, of reflect. Zone for denial, for ignorance.
Zone of the people—of some people. Zone building itself
up all around, becoming edifice. Becoming iron and bars and
shackles. *Free everybody in the chain gang.* Zone of just listen again.
Zone of how did we get here? Zone of how do we get back?
Zone of *They know better, they know better.*

MURIATIC

"My color just comes with
the territory." —Simone Mtanuel

It's 1994 and I'm focused on the kickboard, toes
lipping over pool's edge, anticipating the cool
Anaheim water beneath, a carefully learned leaning
of my body toward the swim instructor, her arms
open, this white woman's embrace the first in a long line
that I'll learn to trust and fear at the same time, but

today it's 2016 and Flint, Michigan, is boiling
the metal in its water futilely, a bubbling brown,
plastic bottles stacked forklift-high, children
stacking up in hospital wait rooms, sick with
this water they were given against their will like

it's 1964 in St. Augustine, Florida, and rabbis
and blacks are swimming in the Monson
Motor Lodge pool while the manager cups a jug
of muriatic acid—clear and colorless—dumps it
into the water he skirts around, and the sheriff's
men refuse to touch it while they pull bodies out
against their will like it's just another day, but today

it's 1936 and white men guard the pool in Pittsburgh's
Highland Park where black boys come up and ask *Why*
can't we swim? and the white men's boots and clubs
answer them for decades and decades, and today

it's 2006 and the fountain in my high school arcs lukewarm
water, cresting like the arch in my bent back, and just below
to the side I see a rectangle of old caulk, ghost of a fountain
coming from the wall, and my back aches like

it's 1950 and my grandfather is thirsty, so he steps
into the long line, bows his head beneath the "coloreds
only" sign, lips pursed to the slow trickle, though
the fountain is cleaner and stronger for "whites
only," but he doesn't dare meddle with their water today,

in 1973, when the pool at Kennywood closes for good,
and some will blame "integration," and some will blame
"maintenance problems," and some will only know the parking lot
paved over, or the splash of the Pittsburgh Plunge
as it dunks into new waters spraying high in the air like

it's 2005 in New Orleans, and Katrina's waters are either sink
or swim, and the government chooses sink, and far too many
whites say *Why don't they just swim?* and far too many blacks
don't have a choice at all, and hot days go by without help like

it's 1963 and the hoses are on us, and it's 1954 and Emmett
Till can't breathe, and it's every year since then that black people
have known the sting of the water and kept back, kept out,
kept waiting for clean waters, safe waters, until finally

it's 2016 and it's a dead heat in Rio, and Simone Manuel's hand
hits the wall, and a gasp and wide-smiled disbelief hits her face
when a black girl wins a gold medal in the water, and wide-smiled
black girls slip on swimsuits, and little brown and black kids peek
their toes over swimming pools' edges, knowing today,
for the first time, the water can be our home too.

BISHOP ON A SLANT

The story goes the tub ran well past midnight,
and whether for bath or baptism I'll never know,

but for Mom finding me and my sister with water
on our heads, our grandfather kneeling near, hands

cupped below the surface (don't all Methodist
preachers do this?) I don't remember it happening

and that's okay because neither did he—drink or
dementia, it didn't matter, I idolized him, wanted

to wear his purple polyester robes with the black
crosses, loved chess too so I knew how to move

like him, a bishop on a slant, and Mom called him Pop
so we did too, told us stories about him and civil rights

and JFK and MLK, NAACP, something about the Symphony
I really didn't get because I only saw him sit, shuffle,

stand in the hallway counting dollars again and again
like his pockets were vaults, then cross the street

to hail cabs that weren't there, or maybe I'd catch him
alone in the kitchen with a bottle of something dark,

catch him alone in the kitchen whistling to himself, or
alone in the kitchen licking palmfuls of table salt

and, hell, when you're seven and he's seventy
how do you know Alzheimer's when it's living

with you in your childhood house, the same house
where in 1968 (the story goes) white neighbors painted

"NIGGER" on the garage door, black words on white
panes, and Pop left it up, wasn't ready to paint

the whole house yet, but when some people called it
"unsightly" he said *I live inside, so the rest of you*

have to live with that word on the outside—which is
funny 'cause most of the whites in the neighborhood had

pooled their money to buy it first, but I guess Pop's pockets
were deep, deep, deeper than the drinks I saw Mom catch him with

and pour down the sink until the whole kitchen smelled
like his breath, which smelled like the green bottles

of aftershave he kept in the bathroom cabinet and rubbed on his face
so I would try it too and panic at the sting on my cheeks,

but thought that's just what shaving felt like, even though
I was too young to grow hair I did it every so often until

his hospice, his deterioration, his death, the September sunlight
I remember draping over his coffin's copper capstone, the sting

of touching the penny-colored block, my thumbprint pressed
permanently on its surface, and you can bet I was scared:

how do you reconcile death with a fingerprint and how
do you reconcile the word "grandfather" with an old man

in your house wearing two pairs of glasses—one for his face
and one for his forehead—how do you reconcile him trying

his best to remember, but still messing up and calling you
by the family dog's name with the fact that he loved you

and your siblings more than he was ever capable of explaining,
how do you reconcile the word "forgiveness" with

the lawyer who brought Pop booze in his hospital bed,
then doctored his will and started siphoning money

from it before you even turned eighteen and realized
why Mom always hid the glass bottles away, why

even the wind of Pop's name had been stiff with bourbon,
but still a name Mom won't ever let die, a name the

city wouldn't let die either, so they carved "Rev. Charles Foggie"
in stone at the corner of Centre and Crawford just so you

could go to college down the block, find it one day and
find out who was really walking around your house

all that time picking his big bent nose, and now you got
that same big bent nose, and now I don't want to say he was a saint

or a sinner or neither, I don't want to say I can see now
how he gave up in later days walking around with anticipation

of the end, and I don't want to use the wrong word for whatever he was,
but all I can say for sure is what happened at dinner most nights,

me and him, seven and seventy, no words at the table, just his fingers
twirling together, in and out of sleeves, behind his back, the sudden

voilà-moment of his empty hands, me watching in awe, never
doubting for a second, both of us believing in his small magic.

FRESH PRINCE

Now this is a story all about how watching *The Fresh Prince of Bel-Air*
you realize you don't know yourself—you know your sister
is Ashley, your cousin is Hilary, your brother is Jazz, your mom

is Aunt Viv (the second one—should have been the first
clue), and you know this from the palms outside their house
that look like the palms around your block, and the palms

of their hands are two-toned like your palms and your hands,
and that bald, big-bellied Uncle Phil bears an uncanny
resemblance to your father, and Bel-Air

bears an uncanny resemblance to your childhood
city, but you don't know who you are so you assume
you are Will: soft smile, smooth talk, ripe reflection

of the kind of blackness you wanted—watched
The Fresh Prince growing up in Orange County while
Will started off *In West Philadelphia, born and raised,* but you

were born in Fullerton, and raised in Pittsburgh,
and mostly around white kids, which made it easy to be
the black one, easy to assume you're the black one

in everything they knew and saw; hard to know
why they loved *Fresh Prince* so much when it was
really just a show about your life; hard to figure out

what any other kid could have seen in your life
that you couldn't—*Chillin' out maxin' relaxin' all cool*
in your corduroy pants and crew neck sweaters,

new electronics under the Christmas tree every year,
braces to set your whole mouth straight, the lecture
Dad gave you about do-rags one time even though

it was a bandana he found in your laundry, the lecture
Dad gave about grillz even though you never wanted any,
(wondering to yourself who made Dad the family judge)

the big, clean house holding all of it together—couldn't
other kids see that you were Will: Nia Long-dating, class
clown, inner city steez with your no rule breaking, no

back-talking, articulate bookworminess, late-night poetry
writing stanza after stanza, asking *Do I really know
myself?* like the page was a mirror and the reflection

you began to see was Carlton: clean-cut Poindexter but darker-
skinned, Philip Banks-protégé however resistant, college-bound
from birth and broken like a horse of a son, not a daring

bone in your body, though your heart beat with the bravado
of a defiant Philadelphian or the eloquence of his silver-tongued
cousin, and it's so hard to tell—you don't know yourself until

you watch the episode when Will and Carlton get trapped
together on the side of a mountain and you realize the mountain
is a place behind your ribs, and the two of them are shades

of the same black boy who has been dueling himself inside you,
season after season, and you begin to question if you've had it
backward this whole time; while Will goes east to west coast you go

from Cali to PA, and while Will's passing time in cool places
you are making yourself cool and passable in white spaces,
pleasing your family, and it's not until you've watched a thousand

hours of the show, until the phrases "Fresh Prince" and "model
minority" become close cousins, until you see how the Banks boys
didn't understand Phil's southern roots—Selma soldier, Watts

witness—that you question if you've ever been that black
that Will brings to Bel-Air (*making trouble in my neighborhood*)
or even eastbound Carlton black, prepped and primed

for Princeton (*I got in one little fight and my mom got scared*)—
it only clicks when you realize you were always more Carlton
and that it's okay; when you realize Uncle Phil loved both boys

to death and stood as a model minority for both of them, so you
could reconcile that "Fresh Prince" is just a name for the love
both boys seek from the judge, just an inheritance every black boy

seeks for himself, and it only clicks when a poem about a TV show
becomes a way of telling your father: *I didn't always understand, and
I still don't always understand, but I'm starting to see a bit better.*

EULOGY FOR THE CONFEDERATE BATTLE FLAG

You kept your thirteen stars even as you flew for only four of them. How brave
of you. On windless days, the red in you hangs a familiar way
from the highest poles white hands could erect. I know why the blue of you
intersects like cold veins searching for the way back to the heart.
You don't need to tell me: you have always been a symbol of an old way of life,
an unwelcome piece of heritage. When your hoisters tell me you don't

stand for that, I laugh because my grandfather dedicated his ministry
to civil rights, marched in southern states where your rebirth burst open black
churches and lunch counters, where blue blood and red blood clashed, and that
is why Pop's bishop robes hold black crosses against a purple
Methodist mantle. You see, heritage is just another word for what you stand for
and stand against. And you stand for the sting of slavery

that was so hot on the backs of my father's ancestors that they fled
into the heart of Canada where ten-foot snow bleached their blackness away
until they could walk with whites who never knew negroes could be anything
but what they saw in the papers, and that is the reason I was raised
to be articulate. You see, articulate is just another way of saying dignity. But
you know that. You know Sumter, South Carolina, is still hot

with the sprint-steps of my great grandfather James, who struck a white man
refusing to pay for the horseshoes James installed, beat the man until he ran
to town and called a lynch mob, and James left his wife and children and ran
to Boston. Dear Battle Flag: this is why I am here. Dear Battle Flag: I was one
rope and branch away from being. Dear Battle Flag: an X is the signature
of an uneducated man. Dear Battle Flag: let me educate you—if you stand

for heritage, why is your heel in the neck of mine, why do I still see your heel
in the necks of my people, why don't you see my people are fed up
to their necks, in need of healing? Dear Battle Flag: how do you execute
the executioner? Does the gravedigger dig his own plot? Dear Battle Flag:
you have brought my people down long enough—today I bring you down.

POST-RACIAL AMERICA: A POP QUIZ

Problem 1

A black boy is killed at 10:27 a.m. News cameras arrive on the scene in twice the time as police backup, which is 1/4th the time it takes to tape off a perimeter. At 11:00 a.m. the first cameras show pictures of a black body face down in the street. At 11:08 a.m. a black man approaches the body and is backed away by an officer to the yellow tape, where the rest of the black community watches in horror. If the speed of a TV satellite signal is distance over the speed of light, how long will it be before white America begins to feel threatened?

Problem 2

Ferguson, Missouri, is on fire. The black community is livid. Looters are looting, arsonists burning, cops in riot gear, citizens in street clothes—in the air: teargas, rocks, glass bottles, and smoke. There are church leaders and police chiefs, teachers and storeowners. At 9:54 p.m. a confrontation begins.

Calculate the sum potential of ethical decision-making in this moment. Compare your results with the class.

Problem 3

Eric Garner, Tamir Rice, Tanisha Anderson, Alton Sterling, Malcolm Ferguson, Rekia Boyd, Michael Brown, Emmett Till, Cameron Tillman, Sandra Bland, Amadou Diallo, Philando Castile, Walter Scott, Renisha McBride, Natasha McKenna, Jordan Edwards, Terence Crutcher, Freddie Gray, Aiyana Stanley-Jones, Trayvon Martin.

Solve for n, where n is the sum of other names you don't know.

Problem 4

Truc or false: Hands Up, Don't Shoot is a prime number.

Problem 5

Jane is white and abhors police brutality. But she thinks the slogan "Black Lives Matter" is too polarizing, even racist. So she writes a post about "All Lives Matter" which gets 279 Facebook "likes." Twice the number of her white friends liked her post as her non-white friends, once the category of her non-white friends is subdivided to exclude Asian Americans, Native Americans, Indians, Hispanics, Latinxs, Pacific Islanders, and Middle Easterners, leaving only Jane's African American friends (in order to present a simpler dichotomy).

Question: what is the absolute value of y, where y is *"All Lives Matter"*?

Problem 6

Which weighs more: a pound of "Black Lives Matter" profile pictures or a pound of solidarity?

Problem 7

Ohio State's football team wins a national championship. Eighty-two percent of the student body is white. Ninety-one percent of the student body celebrates by marching, lighting fires, breaking into the home stadium and vandalizing it. Determine what percentage of the student body consists of "revelers" and what percentage consists of "thugs." Check your math against the results of Problem 2.

Problem 8

There are *c* cops in America, which is four times less than there are unarmed black men. Assuming *b* represents the total number of bullets in the country, how much of *b* will it take before *c* no longer has a job to do?

Problem 9

A middle school girls' basketball team wears *I can't breathe* T-shirts during warm-ups. A picture is posted on Facebook. Group A likes the T-shirts. Group B thinks they're racist. Assume racism is a quantity: 2/3rd of comments blame black deaths on lack of accountability and personal responsibility; 5/8th bring up white people murdered by black youths as a counterargument; 3/5th blame Obama; and 3/10th call it "fad activism." If *t* equals the total number of commenters, use the following equation:

$$r = z^2 \div t$$

Set *z* as a function of "rightness," then solve for *r*, where *r* is the first group past the pole and thus the most oppressed group. Double-check your work.

Problem 10

If the price of free speech is *m*, and people's opinions are *t*, write an equation in which Black *m* might finally be equal to White *t*.

Bonus Question

Solve for *x*, where *x* is the root of the problem.

REUNION

Is this where we started? Zinfandel,
        sea foam,   wet skin,
            those shoes. My throat
     is a beehive. The slack in your bones
looks like someone
                hammocked you together,
     and it's been years
          since I've slept. You are snared
to the night   half-human   a constellation
          of the dimmest stars.
When we talk   your lips cradle
     words like gum bands
     around dead lettuce.   I do not
 mind.   The smell of you
     is everywhere. A chain is dragging
through the palm   of my tongue. There is no
     stopping it. I find a lighthouse
       where your belly belongs.
At the top   a slow fountain
     leaks everywhere.   At the bottom
       coastline
in high-tide shadow.   Outside, a beach
     of skipping stones skipping
back to shore.

BABY,

I'm scared our kids will come out splotchy, my girlfriend, M, texted me
after we spent the morning naming—was it four or five boys
she wanted?—after my thumbs grew numb from exchanging
ideas from opposite ends of campus, and if you're thinking
that I went off and ended our relationship on the spot, you're wrong,
because I pretended I never got the message, and when she didn't
bring it up again after I got to the library, we slipped into a steady study,
since it was November, and finals were coming up, and we became
a new twist on that age-old American vision of college, two kids right
out of MLK's Dream speech, and the point is I saw the list
of baby names doodled down the margins of her notes, clusters
of hearts, and another boy's name we hadn't discussed,
one I knew—and the point is I bought her coffee when it got late
and spit out requisite *I love yous* whenever we'd look up from our work,
my girlfriend thinking mixed children were our biggest threat,
which I guess she could because I didn't teach her what being black
and spotted means, that it isn't the melanin sales reps stalk in stores,
and it isn't the melanin they pull the trigger for, and because
I wanted love then too much for my own good, I could only wonder
if she would become the kind of white woman who'd pull her children
close to her when they saw albino blacks in public, the security
of a caucasian kid yanking at her heart, or if she would learn to let herself
be filled with humility, but more importantly, would I become the kind
of black man who believes dignity is worth more than affection, or
that there's a love where they coexist, though I'm not sure I'm there yet, but
regardless, M, wherever you are now I want to let you know I got your message,
but I pretended it never came because I didn't want you to cheat
on me or cheat on your test—which you did anyway.

SOLEMN PITTSBURGH AUBADE

There are houses on fire every night here. It doesn't seem a sin
                    to let them burn. It doesn't scare me
to wake up to their ghosts still hanging skyward—a siren in the War
                    Streets, its doppelgänger spotted in Garfield
clear across this city, tucked tight between smokestacks smacked
                    along every shore, barge-brown rivers
in a slow grind against the Allegheny plateau. Nothing much changes here.
                    It was built this way and it was built to burn—
I like it like that. After all, what is water without steel to cross it,
                    a mountain that you cannot pierce,
a city without forest all around? Here is where autumn comes to die
                    on stone steps and gridless, potholed streets.
I spend my days by a cathedral watching traffic swell and swirl. I spend
                    my time like a poem spends its lines
trying to find where to pause and where to stop. Most endings
                    and pauses I find can hurt. One time,
I loved somebody. One time, I crossed this street when I was in love.
                    Time will damage anything if you let it,
so we've built this place to last, placed placards of history along the streets,
                    and landmarked any building that dares to crumble.
This is Pittsburgh: black and gold bones buried deep, dinosaurs
                    at cobblestone intersections wrapped in scarves,
hundred-ton iron ladles frozen in shopping districts—we only fight each other
                    about what doesn't get to stay. Sometimes
on these stone steps, I fight myself about what to keep and what to remember.
                    My heart is a museum where all the exhibits
are closed. Love in this city comes as often as the sun, the reset of September
                    pulling clouds over Mount Washington
where I lived and worked, where some nights I'd walk its edge and see
                    houses burning on the horizon, and feel
the flames in my chest. I didn't have a word for it then. All I knew
                    was the feeling of coming home in the evening

to my roommate on his computer watching videos of chess masters
                    playing each other, the silence of him
slumped sideways on the sofa, stacks of Nietzsche and Jung casting shadows
                    on half-full-half-empty coffee cups, eyes heavy
with the shade of the room, a reflection of Bobby Fisher in his glasses,
                    hand on the rook and my roommate's hand
on the trackpad—history with the slide of a finger.

HOW TO HEAL A BOY'S FEVER

"It's hard to dream when your water ain't clean." —Lecrae

Let him dream peace is a blue ship beneath
          the sea where prisoners linger willingly
      swimming warm water circles with one arm
            do not blush or say
    Clouds are almost as blue
        he is not yet a man like you
             some things must be slow
    for his smile to remember itself
or quickly broken into sweat
        if he comes to you
          surrounded by an ocean of sleep
             let him sail it
        star-like and liquid voiced
          crying as if to explore dark skies
      listen when your son asks you
        Father, what makes time so long?
    And why doesn't the sun have two moons
        but always wants more shadows?

FIREFLY

This summer belongs to the little lamps without gravity, flickering
            in and out of the night faster than the stars. I watch them dance
across the grass like constellations coming alive. For so many summers
            this is all I've had, Dad. Tonight I pull out the old chessboard—
black plastic bishops snapped, teeth on rooks' crowns cracked.
            You set your pieces, handing me the black ones as always.

Even as a boy you made me go last, taught me some games
            take patience. I could never defeat you. Back then I once asked
where the light in a bulb came from. You told me great people
            went to the sky and caught enough stars to make the earth glow;
stars that couldn't be tamed became fireflies. Every summer we played chess;
            you never let me win. At times between moves, the board held dust

like snowfall. I'd sit outside and name the fireflies, never telling you
            about all the constellations I found. I didn't want you to know
I was studying their swift light, how I was learning the patterns:
            quick flash, long smolder, how long before the flickers
matched up, then fell apart. I used to wonder if light ever grew tired
            of moving faster than anything. Now, after a quarter of my life,

I still don't know where the stars belong. We revisit these
            broken pieces: white pawn, black knight, white bishop, black king.
You give the same stale opening moves, and in an hour I've beaten you.
            You turn to leave, still not letting me win. I have learned all there is
to patience. I want to take everything you think you taught me and teach you
            what I have learned.

BLACK LOCUSTS

There are no gardens in my neighborhood,
just three black locust trees
in my backyard.
All spring, cream-white petals
blooming like baby teeth,
nectar drooling from the center.
In the summer they stand
as if for a portrait,
lined up like siblings
in the corner of my window.
I grow fond of how they bend
toward each other.
By autumn they droop
and withdraw like moody teens,
leaving all their trash behind them.
They are the children I pray every night to have.
In western Pennsylvania
three seasons go by in a day.
I'm used to it.
I take the leaf blower to their bases,
a stay-at-home father cleaning out
and rearranging rooms while empty-nesting,
whistling all the while.
Later, when winter comes,
I watch kudzu creep up their trunks,
wrapping itself over every inch,
stealing away the last bits of sun.
Before the first snowfall I'll sharpen a hatchet,
read up on girdling, stand at the window,
and wonder which sort of death they deserve.

IF A BAG OF SILVER COINS AND
A BAG OF BULLETS SOUND THE SAME

then take my ears   I do not need them
                    and if America can look
a muzzle in the face and not see
            its own hand behind the barrel
                        then take my eyes   I do not want them
        and if prayers no longer suffice then take
my lips and undo my tongue   from its moorings
        Lord take each part of me back
                    until You don't recognize my image

            What is the opposite of a kiss
anyway? There will be no lice or locusts
                no boils or bloodied rivers to tread
        no frogs or fire or firstborns doomed   Leave me
my palms and know if I put them up to the sky
            I am asking to be filled
not with lead   but with Your love

        A bible group hummed some holy hymnal
        before the evening ran red   A gun hummed
        nine death notes and I watched You catch
        each one   What is the opposite of mercy?

Delusions of white power   higher than Sinai
        Lord leave me something to ache
                    for those souls delivered
too soon   What is there to do   but cover
        your neighbor as you would have them
                cover you? What more will You take
        of me? I am sick up to my neck

but if You leave my arms
            I will climb flagpoles

while the people say   *Goodbye Rhodesia*
goodbye Klan   goodbye red mantle   and star-shackled blue bars
          If America is   some promised land
let me be the ocean's highest tide   Mother

          will not drown   The people cry
                    Emanuel!
so You must be here   They are not afraid
          to be Your lighthouse of hope   In the name
of Thy Son let me fill the church to the steeple
                and I will wash sin and spilled blood alike
          And if water is rebirth   Lord make my flood holy

AN HONEST PRAYER

I don't know why I close my eyes and lace
         my fingers like the seam of a baseball just
to whisper into palm lines what I have wanted

         to scream all day. My black cross
is faded on the edges, not from prayer
         but wear beneath shirts grown tight

from too much eating. What comes across my plate
         I can only stomach so much, and night
is when I confess what I wish

         someone would ask me. Yes, there are people I no
longer speak to who still cause me fire; yes, there's
         a hole in my wallet I cannot seem to stitch;

yes, there's a grandchild I owe my parents still
         not conceived. In the cold I grow a beard as if
it's my job, think of the bible, speculate about

         if Genesis had just been it and we didn't worry
about doing all the rest. There's a person in the clouds
         my prayers pass right through. Hard to bat

away these thoughts of missing old friends
         and shitty lovers despite their shittiness;
these thoughts less spirit, more radio-wave,

         dialogue of electron and magnet. A poet
tells me mourning is meditation, but what zen
         is there in a gaunt heart not even my blood wants

to flow back to? Maybe attachment is a red herring,
         or a slow hand job I can't tell if I want to keep

going or to end. Yes, I believe loss is an intimacy

strong enough to shake legs and roll tongues
and eyes deep into skulls. So, here's a prayer method:
first, base pleas in something concrete; second,

wait for the urgency to harden; third, think of hope as a way
to push in a literal sense. Tonight, I pray for a home
to never run from, a warmth that is more shadow

than stubborn shade, for paper cuts on that lover's
finger—because I don't know how to pray in absolutes,
or in a sequence that leads to enlightenment

or renaissance or brimstone, but I know
that with every swing of the tongue
over my teeth, I'm getting closer.

NOTES ON CAMERON BARNETT

I remember that I'm black
on occasion: when there's paperwork
or shopping to be done, when
somebody is shot in America
and the nation holds its breath
till the shooter is identified, when
I kiss the woman I love
in public and imagine watching
from another person's perspective,
when a car bangs rap music
down the street and I can hear
a passerby mutter *Niggers*
under her breath.

***

The palms of my hands are lighter than the backs,
a clear line running down each finger—the same
with my feet, the same with my arms. At the base
of my neck there's light skin in the shape of a Y
like post-autopsy stitching. I am a living swirl.

***

My full name is Cameron Bryce Barnett. I will often tell you
my name sounds very white—I will never tell you my name
doesn't sound black enough.

***

Everything you see in me is a ghost story.

Everything I see in you is scripture.

Everything we see in each other is a constellation.

***

In 11th grade a friend asked me if my semen was black like me. I reminded him how often he called me *The whitest black guy he knew.*

***

In my junior year of college I was accused of plagiarism for using the term "en media res" in a paper. The professor told me it was an A paper, then confronted me on the term. After I defined it for him, he waited another week and gave me the paper back—a B.

***

In my junior year of college I was accused of cheating on a quiz which I took in front of the professor in her office, the answers for which she had sent the class in advance. She confronted me days later, pressing me to confess. She did not appreciate how I stood my ground. *Cameron...* she said like a weary parent, head cocked—*What?!* I bellowed, water gathering in my eyes.

***

Everything black about me is an heirloom.

Everything white about me is a blueprint.

Everything I love about me fits in a palm.

***

I have often believed character is a faucet
and personality is like water. I have often
found myself running a faucet for minutes
at a time, hands already cleaned. I have often
scrubbed my hands to the point that I
no longer care for my skin.

***

Occasionally, a friend of mine likes to point out that all of my relation-
ships have been interracial. *What's up with that?* he asks with a smirk.
Which to hate more: the question or the smirk?

***

I have the darkest skin in my family, while my brother gets mistaken
for white. My mother and sister: palettes of beige, buff, and brown.
In the summer my father is almost my color. It isn't really the shade
of my skin that bonds me to family. I didn't make this body black, curl
this hair, plump these lips—but I did learn how to carry this body,
where to put it, how to explain its presence anywhere.

***

I want to say life comes in more colors than we know—that those who
"don't see" aren't unlike those who look too close.

***

What does white privilege look like in a black body?

***

I often step off the curb to go around white people
coming down the sidewalk. I don't even have to
think about it. I know they won't move for me, and
I don't want purses to be afraid I'll snatch their women.

***

I learned how to juggle at the age of eight, the same age I was
when I learned how to moonwalk. These are more than metaphors
for how to get through life, they are tricks I am asked to perform
time and again once people find out I can do them—this
is a metaphor for blackness.

***

Another black poet told me he liked my poem
for Emmett Till despite *His story being overdone.*
For weeks I fantasized about switching out
the murderers' names and putting in his.

***

When I say I do not care for my skin, when I say I wanted to get rid of
it, when I say it has given me everything, when I say it does nothing for
me, when I say I am numb, when I say I don't see my own race, when I
say it sees me, when I say every consequence carries a color, when I say
you can have it, when I say it is mine...what do you hear?

ACKNOWLEDGMENTS

Many thanks to the editors who first published some of these poems (some in different versions):

Barely South Review, Blast Furnace, City Paper: Chapter & Verse, Lexicon Magazine, the Florida Review, Ghost Town, Green Hills Literary Lantern, Lines + Stars, the Minnesota Review, Off the Coast, the Pittsburgh Foundation, Pittsburgh Post-Gazette, Pittsburgh Poetry Houses, Pittsburgh Poetry Review, Pretty Owl Poetry, Rattle, TriQuarterly, and *Winter Tangerine Review.*

Thank you to my friend and fellow writer, Nina Sabak, for the title inspiration.

Thank you to Terrance Hayes, Yona Harvey, Lynn Emanuel, and Nick Coles for your guidance in my graduate work and the earliest versions of this book.

My deep appreciation to the talented and caring poets and writers at Pitt, without whom the shape and existence of many of these poems would not be possible. Most especially thanks to Kimberly Grabowski Strayer for your sincere love and attention to every poem I sent your way, and to Malcolm Friend for being a brother to me and showing me how to be fearlessly proud and black.

My love to my family and friends with whom I've shared these poems and who read and believed in this work all along, sometimes before I did.

My never-ending gratitude to all the teachers who helped me learn to love books and writing, most especially: David Ross, Greg Wittig, Katherine Wilkins Bienkowski, Linda Kinnahan, and Craig Bernier.

Many thanks to editors Alison Taverna and Christine Stroud for the production of this book.

"Supernova" and "Skin Theory" are written for and after my friend, the poet Kimberly Grabowski Strayer; the poems in the "Note Broker" series come from a collection *The Bones We Lose,* which takes up the project of Yusef Komunyankaa's Thorn Merchant series; "Black Locusts" is written after Alison Seevak; "The Wife" ends with lines borrowed from Ludwig Wittgenstein; "Between Skin" is written after John Straley; "Baby," is written after Terrance Hayes; "Smoke" is written after Larry Levis; "Emmett Till Haunts the Library in Money, MS" is written after John Berryman; "No Flex Zone" is written after Kristin Naca; "Solemn Pittsburgh Aubade" begins with lines borrowed from Scott Silsbe.

2016 & 2017 Releases

St. Francis and the Flies by Brian Swann Winner of the 2015 Autumn House Poetry Prize, selected by Dorianne Laux

Bull and Other Stories by Kathy Anderson Winner of the 2015 Autumn House Fiction Prize, selected by Sharon Dilworth

Presentimiento: A Life in Dreams by Harrison Candelaria Fletcher Winner of the 2015 Autumn House Nonfiction Prize, selected by Dinty W. Moore

Glass Harvest by Amie Whittemore

Apocalypse Mix by Jane Satterfield Winner of the 2016 Autumn House Poetry Prize, selected by David St. John

Heavy Metal by Andrew Bourelle Winner of the 2016 Autumn House Fiction Prize, selected by William Lychack

RUN SCREAM UNBURY SAVE by Katherine McCord Winner of the 2016 Autumn House Nonfiction Prize, selected by Michael Martone

The Moon is Almost Full by Chana Bloch

Vixen by Cherene Sherrard

The Drowning Boy's Guide to Water by Cameron Barnett Winner of the 2017 Rising Writer Prize, selected by Ada Limón

For our full catalog please visit: http://www.autumnhouse.org